To Travel Without a Map

Poems by, K. A. Brace

Published by, *Mirror Obscura Publications Inc.*

This book is dedicated to:

Mac Sawyer Hammond
"The brown thrush, the dark wave"

And

Richard L. Demarco
The better angel of my nature.

With special thanks to:
Gerry (*Gypsy*) Taylor

Table of Contents

The Things That Happened

To Travel Without a Map

The Situation of Gravity

The Way Water Freezes

The Importance of Wonder

The Things That Happen

The Things That Happen

Very often it means nothing. The mechanicalness of clocks
Justifies itself by filling the empty moment that occurs when
You turn to the next page in your book. A piece by *Glass* comes
To mind, reminding you to get flowers for her birthday, then
                                        Slips away.

From her balcony she can see the lives of the block
Take place. 'Los Terribles,' they call themselves, play
Hide and seek. Now, it is the youngest one who must find.
A boy climbs into an old ice-box. The door closes. He will
                                        Not be found.

Three blocks away a priest is hearing confessions' drone.
A woman tells him she has sinned against God, by sleeping
With a member of the cloth. He leans closer to the screen. Softly,
He says to go on, forgiveness in his voice. He knows what he
                                        Needs to hear.

In a basement apartment, barely lit from outside, a young
Couple argue, how could this happen, they cannot afford
To have this child making its way into their lives. Frustrated
The man slaps her hard across the face. Later as he sleeps,
                                        She leaves forever.

On her lunch hour a widow sits, in the park reading Nabokov
In Russian, she laughs out loud. A man who has loved her
For twenty years walks by. They have never spoken. He stops,
Hesitates, 'It must be funny.' Looking up into his eyes, she asks
                                        Him to please sit.

On the subway for the first time the boy grips his father's hand.
They are going to see a baseball game, another first in this day
Of firsts. They must change lines. His father sweeps him up into
His arms. Closer to his father's heart he thinks, nothing else matters,
                                        Even if the Yankees win.

Einstein Meets with God

'This beach is much better,
Less radiation. Alamogordo?
Was that supposed to be a joke?
Attitude? Yes, I suppose so.
But at my age I can afford one.
It's not news to you–our relationship
Has always been iffy. Yes I know
All about the train schedules.
But you knew what I was thinking.
Besides, I did all the work and
Was abused for it—after all I'm not
Your son. Why this meeting? Now?
I didn't want to wait until after…
Why? To ask you: Hiroshima? Nagasaki?
What did you think would come of it all?
Tell me please, dear God,
There was a plan after all.'

The Rose Trees

The beginnings of his invisibility began for her
As he pointed out the brilliance of the fall
In the still chilled threatening frostair of spring.
One morning she woke to find him ambling
Down the walk, his arms upraised, his once
Strong hands combing the leaves of her rose trees.
She heard him singing a favored childhood song.
In between the simple verses he stopped and laughed
From deep within his nakedness for all to see.

Through the year, after each visit to the doctor
She began to see more and more of him not to see.
At home, as each day became the next, he became
Tenderness obsessed with the rose trees he'd planted
On her birthday that first year, now a lifetime ago.
She watches him move among them, circling each one,
the tips of his fingers caressing their barks
Like a blind man reading a history in braille.

As she watches him now, she saw him then, taking
Long strides to measure where each hole was to go.
On his hands and knees drawing perfect circles
All by eye, exact diameters, a high druid priest
Ensuring ever perfect growth by incantations of
Raw toil, blisters and the work of three days in heat.
She would watch him from the veranda, shirtless,
Sweat and focused muscles in a graceful masculinity.
With all twelve thin saplings planted, 'Straight as
The God damned Pyramids!' he yelled, calling her.

Stepping from shade into his light, recognizing
The gleam of living life in his eyes, their depths
Of passion, the smile that had wrapped around her
The first time he had spoken to her, not hearing a word.

The Rose Trees continued…

Now summer's drought has screamed their lives out.
The trees' stark twisted branches, upraised,
Implore some god to make the rain come.
No gods are listening. Axe and saws end in fire.
Gone into ashes just as he is now only an outline;
A man whose last hold in his world she visits is
One focused curiosity, "The rose trees?" He asks.
"How are the rose trees?" She holds a hand
She barely knows, tells what she always sees in him,
Of the infinity of blossoms on each one, each
And every one of the dozens of times he asks.
Not even aware that she is there, asking anyone.

One day she knows she will come and all there will
Be left of him will be his impression on the pillow.
Then, she will sit, look at the pillow and tell it
About a man, with a smile so like an Apollo,
Who planted rose trees everywhere he went and so
Pleased the Gods they made his trees bloom year round
And welcomed him into their company forevermore.

If Dogs Could Talk

It's not hard to feel that every dog
I ever had extended me the privilege
To have been loved. That is what
They show us; why, no doubt,
God created them to begin with.

Sit, fetch, roll-over, play-dead, are tricks,
As well as other things, they let us teach
Because they know how good it makes
Us feel about ourselves.

But, being joyful cannot be taught.
Or, to somehow know your car has
Turned the last corner for home.
Then wait impatiently to greet you,
As though you'd been gone for years.
Or, to curl around your feet to sleep
As if that spot were the most comfortable
Of beds they could have found.

Just as, you cannot teach them the trust
That you must earn, for them to tell you
At the end with a fading look they know
Their time has come.

I believe, if dogs could talk,
They would tell us, in a soothing
Whisper, that it's them
Who'll miss you more, just so it will
Not break your heart to see them go.

A Rural Story

It's not a place Wyeth would have come
To paint in taupe, faded green and gray.
The house and barn gutted over with ash
And charcoal rippled timbers, two naked
Chimneys pointed skyward far above
Where the roofline lay now, charred and split
In two, caved-in onto what was a living space.

Here great grandparents sat, succeeded
By the next in line, generations overlapped,
Pages intermingled in a book begun beyond
Breathing memory, and watched the newness
Of life take part in who they were as family
--Births, deaths, loving, some disappearing,
Swallowed up by a world far from fences,
Fields and warnings before leaving Home.

Now, none are left to pass secrets down.
Or, hand down hand-me-downs, tell stories
About some things remembered that never
Really happened, or give over heirlooms,
Precious in simply being gifts of ritual.

As years pass the land too will change.
None will be recalled by step, or laugh,
Or acts of kindnesses or, by name.

Ice Skating

Some years, winter is so hard it brings a snap
To everything, the snow surface under foot,
A dog's bark, the air, your breath, the sun.
At least it seems that way out here where
No rush of city background noise deafens
Whispers and there are still woods and ponds
That no one owns, or claims to want to.

As if the word were in the air, after it's been
Cold long enough and the first snow less than
A few days down, packed tight in its weight
With a quiet only this season bears, it begins.

A young boy with a shovel tentatively tests
The edge-ice of the pond with his boot.
Pushing harder each time until confident
It will hold; he steps out onto the white
Covering and begins, bit by bit to clear the ice.
Soon two more arrive, put skates on, grab
Their shovels, test the ice like ritual, before
Beginning farther down to clear a pathway
Out to the middle and slowly make a circle,
Ever widening it shovel full by shovel full.

By mid-morning more than a dozen souls
Are on the pond, big pylons of snow placed
Across the southern end which never seems
To thick-freeze no matter how cold it gets.
Noon comes, all shoveling done, an ad hoc
Hockey game is underway and an unofficial
Area designated by the growing crowd
All moving counter-clock wise in an oval,
As if collectively they can turn back time.

Couples talk low and intimate about later.
Others shouting hellos to one another
Across the middle, where those more skilled
And adventuresome make figure 8's going
Backwards, cutting them smaller, smaller,
Tighter. Then, stop--tipped on toe points,
Frozen—to burst off in slicing speed, skating
Along the outer rim of the infield ice going
Clockwise, against the crowd, as if moving
Faster into the future than they really are.

A Death in the Family

Yesterday, in the common hours, a woman was dead.
The heart, in pain, gave in and what was recognized
As her animation had departed.
It happened elsewhere.
In cities, along country roads, in fields,
Back and forth down the random streets
Of various states. The scenery changed little more
Than it might have otherwise, but for the presence
Of an absence that begins to settle on the furniture
And marks the snapshot-present forever in the past.
There, in those separate but concerted places,
In the widening gulf on the outward voyage,
Between ship and state, the allegory in the journey
Ceased its relativity and became valid.

In the living great and near-great,
Among the poets and potentates of power,
In the halls of governments and bureaucracies of art,
Death's omnipresence is accepted.
The moment need only happen.
We are attuned to the failure of our instruments
To predict the unassailable. We note the intricacies
Of the dials' delineations and give way to those
Who read the meanings in the graphs and charts
That they compile. The loom and shuttle become
Mere icons. We recall Chance,
The cutting of the thread, in what was said
In the color of the clouds,
In the coincidences of where we were.
For a brief instant we are called upon to question
If the laws of nature alone suspend the bridge
Across the river.

A Death in the Family continued...

But, in the small deaths, in the human, in the many,
As they occur together in their singular moments,
The temperature continues, unrecorded
To voice the climate.
Whenever it happens it is a cruel month.
The world shrinks into the smallest of spheres.
We are met by the silence that allows
Tragedy in the theatre to exist. In the rising footlights
The houselights' flickering off,
We never know the pain.
We only recognize its hurt in others
And in the particular way the snow falls, listless,
On the cars moving fast, precarious
                        And past us.

The Globe Umbrella

In a rainy city for the day I stop
Inside the lobby of a high rise icon,
Shake the rain off, check the time,
Watch the street to wait the downpour
Out. It's funny what people use when
They forget, or never carry, an umbrella:
Newspapers, plastic bags, briefcases,
One man used a small oriental rug.

Rain is different in the country,
Less a nuisance. If you don't have
An umbrella you just get wet. But here,
People hurry as if that will be some help.
Like people getting lost when driving.
They tend to go faster as if the way
Home is past some finish line. I check
The time again, I've got no choice.
But, as I exit the revolving door,
Out of the corner of my eye, surrounded
By a sea of makeshift umbrellas,
A man is balancing, on his head a large
Globe of the earth. I wonder,
Maybe it would stop raining here
If he would only turn the world around.

That Day

That day was ordinary, in its way so much
Like any other. The sun unimpressed
Hung at its zenith as the population,
Patrician, plebian and freedman alike slow
To rouse given to excesses at the revelries
Of the Vulcanalia, praise to a fire god no one,
Yet still dreaming, could imagine dwelt inside
The mountain shadowing a city and its harbor.

A jeweled spot, spotted tight with villas
Of the rich vacationing from Rome – Time
Away from the heat of her streets and Forum
A blessing when bathed by cool airs flowing
Off clear blue waters of the Tyrrhenian,
On that day in late August in sweet Pompeii.

Early grapes, picked and pressed were already
Fermenting, casks and barrels stored in cellars.
Gladiators sat in their school's yard some
Praying, giving thanks to Nemesis their god
For protection and deliverance as they tended
And rebound wounds, muscles flexing with
Stiffness from the games fought yesterday.

In the Lupanar *exotic* women, some just girls,
Washed and fixed faces, combed their tresses
In anticipation of early patrons, while on a wall
A young Lucianus scratched dubious graffiti
In vulgare Latinum, extolling the attributes
Of a sister who worked there and kept her
Family barely balanced on the brink of disaster.

The Procurator of the city, Antonius Felix deftly
Left the bed of his mistress, Drusilla, a Jewish
Princess, of provocative demeanor, who was
At that very moment being cursed by his wife
Of thirteen years, across the other side of the city.

That Day continued…

By the harbor wharves, behind the fullones,
A woolier, Vesonius Primus, was just chaining
Up his dog and in a hurry to meet his banker,
Siricos, on whose door lintel was inscribed
Salve, lucre (welcome, money) and had been up
Counting before the sunrise broke into that day.

There were other early risers, visiting merchants
Who sat in the many caponae already drinking
Wine and dipping bread into a fish stew that was
A staple of the Empire's diet. Some laughed in fits
When a shepherd passed them wailing
How his flock of six-hundred fell, almost
All at once, to the ground, not one left breathing,
As if Death's Air had descended from the sky.

Oh! Nona, Decima, Morta. How busy they were
That day in August, spinning, measuring, preparing
To see the many threads be cut, of mortals who
Would find their sacrifices to the gods were
For nothing in the few hours left them, before their
World was buried over and forgotten for 1500 years.

Do you think the Fates feel any? Do they laugh
When such things take place, searing heat and ash
Filling in the grave of so many trapped in simply
Living that day, just like the last, or the next
Had it come to pass? Or, do they just move on
To tend to other lives, leaving only a dark haze,
An air which the sun could not shine through
                                        That day.

Bus Stops

I have watched the woman from down
The block, every day, slowly make her way
To the bus stop, wait for hours, letting
So many busses pass on by.
Finally, the one she has been waiting for comes.
I can hear the hydraulic hiss-pop
Of the door opening accordion fashion
To let her on. Tight with age she steps up,
A too short arm extending past her coat sleeve,
To hold to the rail. The patient driver looks
From under the brim of his cap, willing her
to move quicker and find a seat, waiting
Till she does.

The bus pulls out from the stop,
Diesel fumes roiling swirls a smoke screen
Making traffic back away. The large machine
Continues on its routed way,
Veering to the curb and its next stop.
In a choreographed motion, the impetus
Of energy helps her get up, step into
And down the aisle, to the exit.

She watches the bus move off
And cautiously makes her way
Across the street to sit at the bus stop there,
Once more waiting for the right bus
To come and take her back to her street
So she can walk the block and a half
Back to the flat, she shared
With her sister until she died.

There are those days
When I think more than I should.
I want to go sit next to her
As she waits on the bench and do
All that she does, to experience
How to fill the loneliness
Which echoes inside a heart.

It's nothing you can prepare for
Like the cold, but waits, anticipating,
Until all the busses
Pass on by.

The Ambulance

Each time we fail at love there is an absence
That will not be absent from us.
For a moment all traffic stops.
Life is still-life. The ambulance weaves its way
Down the avenue into the heart of the city.
Its high pitched movement and flashing moan
Seem little more than a trick
In photography. The sky looks like rain,
The air is impassable with the impatience
Of an art museum where, beneath a portrait
By Modigliani, *The Servant Girl*, a woman sits
As if she were the artist's model for life.

It is easy to see. Her eyes drift
Across the ocean of the room
From the body of her island,
Whose inhabitants have never learned
To swim beyond the waves. They know
There is no danger in the water, the swell,
Or in the failing weather of the sea's vastness.
Their fears lie close to shore. Always it is the surf
Where drowning seems less miraculous,
Where dreams are somewhat more than sleep…

The ambulance passes.
The signals change. The cars move on
And we continue, in all our frailties, toward love;
While outside in the beginning rain, umbrellas bloom
Like mushrooms on the damp airs of the street.

Stolen Seconds

(ARBEIT MACHT FREI)

Include the names
Of all who came here
In your diary of daily prayers.

So few are left
That can remember
How permanent the hours
Were made to be,
The minutes elongated
To salt their thirst for
Hope cowed by terror.

So, they stole the seconds
When no one used them.
Kept them,
For themselves,
Like names.

The precious, dire seconds
For themselves to live in.
Hid them behind sunken eyes
That stopped seeing
Because there was
Too much to see.

The secret seconds
No one could confiscate,
Throw onto piles
Like suitcases, shoes,
Eyeglasses and shorn hair.

The cautious seconds
That fed belief the world
Had not gone insane.
That somewhere their names
Were still spoken
Out loud.

Even as the snow of ashes,
Fell delicately to the ground.

"Who's on First"

I smell her scent in the hall first,
Then I see her. She's waiting
For me just like she always does,
With that 'think you're man enough'
Smirk on her face, her left leg thrown
Out like a French hooker–her fantasy.
But it's that hand on her hip
That always gets to me,
There's something about it…
Then, once on the landing there's
That New York touch in her voice,
The foreplay banter, an X-rated
Rendition of Abbott and Costello's
"Who's on First," or, do I 'have
What it takes to make a slide into
Home to score the winning run?'

I tell her that I might be a bad bet
And get sent to the showers.
She just Chuckles, tilts her head so her hair
Covers one eye, smiles and says,
'Let's get wet.'

Always the same game
But every night it's different,
There's the change-up, the fast ball
When you don't expect it.
The crack of the bat and you know
The visiting team just scored in the win column.

It's just coming up on nine years now..
It's like…
I wish to God She were still alive.

How We Say Goodbye

It begins early. A broken bird, frantic,
Caught. Tenderness nesting it inside
A shirt. The shoebox top with holes
For air. The world compressed into
Scratches on cardboard. All night, awake;
Willing it to live on wilted lettuce
And the vigil. But sleep comes. Waking
With a start, to learn how hope grows
Cold to touch. We add guilt to the list
We've started without knowing it.

Primitives knew what loss was.
Embraced it. In their way of life
Death was welcomed. In a universe
Of circles inside of circles,
No beginning, no end, the dead
Did not disappear. They walked where
'The dog ran across the sky.'
All arcs were pathways to becoming
Voices on the wind,
Dreams in sleep, and spirit
Forms of animals, guides for learning
The ways of earth, the stars, of living.

We are loathe to talk of death,
As if dying was a sin.
Hospital rooms are obligations.
People we forgot we knew and
Those we never did, comfort
The sick, and the sicker, the dying.
People mean well. They are plagued
By guilt. Those left behind live
The last moments left as if the dying
                Are doing it on purpose.

How We Say Goodbye continued…

I have been there twice, alone, to watch
The desperate struggles the body makes
Trying to convince the mind
Something terribly wrong is happening.
A mistake has been made somewhere
Along the line, someone, somehow,
In some way erred.

In time, the body has been convinced.
Breathing that was shallow, quick,
Strained, begins to assume a rhythm
It had never had. The breath
Is pulled in deeply, savoring the tastes
Of living, understanding what they are.
Slow motion, the chest relaxes, the breath
Becomes the air again, a sigh of peace,
The circle we deny, descends at last
                            And turns again.

.

The White Heron

A man in middle years, not rich or poor, works
News of the world, selling newspapers, locally
Trades in hellos, goodbyes, pleasantries all day,
But lives among the rich fallacies of truth
In local gossip as a way of life to *sustain*.

Each day, neatly dressed, his pronounced limp,
Proof of courage in a war, takes him up
The same streets to his kiosk, after closing,
The same path home. Mid-way on each sojourn
He stops at his café, for coffee and more gossip.
From his table at the front, he looks out
Across the street, up into a window and sees
The same cobalt blue glazed vase always filled
With fresh cut flowers. He swears, to himself,
He can smell color accented fragrances
All the way from here. He smiles, wonders who?
Nodding in agreement, *Yes, many men go there*.

At sunrise every morning, in a fraying silk robe,
Marie, barefoot, shivers in the chill, gathers
Her choice of flowers for the day. In her small
Apartment, by the window, near the sink.
She takes yesterday's still vibrant blooms
From the vase, wraps their stems in newsprint,
A gift for the old woman who lives next door.

She stands at the window, arranges the day's cuttings
In the, chipped, gold rimmed, blue enamel vase,
Looks out across lush green marshlands, at the mist
That clings and lays light across the grasses, the sun
Halved by horizon this early, and thinks briefly
Of Robert, a man she'd met, just before a war.

The White Heron continued …

There is no window that does not have a view
That isn't seen by someone looking out, or in.
We see or we are seen. Among all possibilities,
The frailties and faults we find in furtive attempts
To know ourselves before others see the wrongs in us.
We smile when we are sad. We stay when we should go.
We busy us mad with details as our hearts
Bid us *breathe slow.*

Out in the marshes to the east nothing strange occurs.
The mist begins to lift within the day's heating air.
A breeze from cool waters offshore, weaves
Into the blades of grasses as they tap and brush
At each other with a rhythmed rhyme.

A white heron glides low over small stands of white
And purple irises, offering their fragility, opening
                                        In its flight.

To Travel Without a Map

To Travel Without a Map

I.

In measured steps of caution,
I have begun to caress my past life
Into the fullness of the present.
Old ground becomes new landscapes
Because I see the enigmatic shapes
Shadows take from the substance
They mimic must still have
Their genesis in light.

Before, that subtly was lost on me,
My focus set on footprints thought
To be signs of someone else ahead
I followed. Tracking myself in circles
I became a lost man stammering,
Who had sinned against himself.
Who had found he could not bear
To hear his own confessions.

I thought the opposite of the light
Was dark, but found the other side
In its purity of intent was nothingness
                    Without surrender.

II.

There is the wandering that comes from timidity
Engendered by being unsure, all confidence
Slowly drained, an ember ashing back, lost.
Across some terrain it is recklessness at anytime
To travel without a map. It is impossible without
Understanding the language your senses speak.
To trust in them is to be sure they will tell you
What they don't know more than what they do.
Anything can become a land mark missed, mistaken,
Or, ignored by over-thought false heroics born
From the fear unwilling to be admitted. Left
Deaf, blind and dumb you stagger under a yoke
Of intuition based on nothing more than
Going in whatever direction the wind has gone,
A vane whose terminus is in its endless turning.

31.

III.

Then, there is the wandering born in the very act
Of acknowledgement that there are always risks.
Here, to not risk is to risk everything at one roll.
The map to this territory is the one you draw inside
Your mind. It is made from mistake and discovery,
Weariness of body and strengthening of heart,
Answering doubt by asking questions, watching
The lines between them fade with exploration. Go
For the sake of going. Searching to know you have
Been there because it is the only thing you can do.

IV.

Even the road to nowhere leads
Somewhere despite what those
Who have not traveled may say.
In the thick scent of pines breath
Becomes your measure of distance
As you evolve unleadened by
The weight of time. In the fog
That fills the valleys the path
Is always clear, always forward.
Memories are more than the ashes
Of the fire that burns inside.
But that flame belongs
To another self you leave behind
With every step by step you take.

The road to nowhere leads
Somewhere, though it may not
Be a place. It could be only
The journey waits for you around
The bend, beyond the hill.
It is the traveler without a map
Who makes destiny a companion
By understanding the differences
Along the way between a heart's
                    Desire and fate.

Locus

We are two points, loci, on an untitled map.
No compass rose to show direction, no relief
Denoting the rise and fall in the terrain.
We might only be opposite slopes of one hill,
Habitué of the same spring waters, moving,
Crisscrossing barely trampled grassy paths.

At once we are undiscovered cities, just
Our selves to count as citizens who meet
To discuss important matters of the day.
Or, we are explorers who will only know
What we are seeking once it's been discovered.

At night we watch the same stars that are no aid
In navigation. We are not lost, neither are we
Found. In a wilderness of intrinsic possibilities
We can send out search parties of only one.

Tonight floats Orion, his stars' light belt circled
Around his girth. If I could just hang there for
A moment I might see a small star like fire's light
And know just where you are. Yet, pondering
Improbables gets us nowhere nearer than where
We are. So, I will think you fair, while you see me old.
Or, you see me brave, and I see you as a nag.
Without speaking let us both agree that if we must
Live as this, we must love to live, so love me
As I will love you as well, wherever we might be.

Collecting

Every departure from my life
Is a particular kind of death
I feel inside. The person
Who I was then slowly slides
Into a history all its own
And all evidence of that reality
Is no longer alive in me.

But fate compensates
In other ways I much prefer.
For instance on another day I find,
While browsing in an antique shop,
A photograph taken in a foreign place
In which the light-fall is so tangible,
The shadows cast so like a voice
Unknown, and yet, familiar.
It is not hard imagining it as a place
I know, and embrace it as a truth
To take the place of a part of me
That died somewhere before.

Truth be told it's not just shops
That are repositories for things
I find to fill the voids.
Sometimes on the street I'll see
An errant playing card,
Perhaps a three of hearts,
A crumpled note telling me
To remember to bring flowers
"Love, M.," no where, or when.

As every day goes by in increments
An item here, a trinket there,
Slowly bit by bit by happenstance
Postcards, matchbooks, foreign coins,
Keys that unlock nothing;
I surround myself with pieces
That I've imbued with memories
Of a life that has never been
And put in place so delicately
As though each moment past
Were an exotic moth I've pinned
To display in a collection I take out
To show myself, a proof, that I exist.

Staying in the Lines

Away from the closeness of houses in town
Ran a new paved two lane blacktop road
That connected us to the great interstate net
Of highways laid down under 'I like Ike,' Ike,
A signal there were places *we* were going.
In the late 50's, the fearless duck and cover
Days of schools, I wore crew cuts, cut by my father,
Ate lunches my mother made for me with care
And learned correct spelling was so important.
There was a column for it on my report card
Right next to the ones that indicated how well
I worked with others and stayed in the lines.

On Tuesdays everyone knew without looking
Circles were colored blue, squares were yellow
And the triangle, which always made me think
Of Pyramids in Egypt and then the Sphinx,
Was always to be colored-in in big bright red.

One Tuesday, I'm sure it was in October,
I thought my work sheet would look better
If, with the other colors, my circle were black.
The next day, in the morning, during recess,
The room phone rang. The teacher answered.
I was handed a message to bring down the hall.

In the office I saw my mother talking to
A man wearing glasses and an unlit pipe smile
On his mouth. He said hello with a too far
Hand extended to introduce himself and
Then guided me into his office where he
Began to ask me what I thought about words
On cards, and drawings. I said the Sunday
Funnies were way much better and he began
To write things on his pad. From then on,
Every Tuesday when everyone in class
Was filling in their circles with crayons
That were blue, I was sitting in his office
Answering the same questions he'd asked
The week before, as if he had forgotten
What I'd told him, as if I'd never been there.

The Map

The river flows south in strong currents
Beneath her window. The winter ice, broken,
Surges in an exodus of small disasters, larger floes
Made smaller, smaller ones, ground
Into their rightful element of river water.

Her tea has grown cold sitting on the black lacquer tray.
She reaches for the cup, black too, but it is
The black that surrounded the stars, when both
She and they were younger. A wisp of still chilled spring
Ruffles the freshly pressed white-laced curtains,
The occasion of a seasonal change. Her fingers touch
The panel of delicate cloth, feels the stork pattern raised,
Imagines their flight, bringers of good fortune,
The wide span of their wings as they glide, the sun
Casting their shadows, rising and falling with the terrain
Below them, giving the false impression
Of tremendous speed.

From the small kitchen comes a clatter and breaking.
She turns. It was the cat being a cat. She sits back
And hopes that the damage was not one of her
Iris with Dragonfly plates, the design she picked,
A wedding gift to him, the year before she went blind.

The world she once saw now lives on the map of her mind.
Every space she traverses runs through a longitude and latitude
Of memory and discovery. Distance is measured by steps.
Her fingers touch the reliefs of every continent she brushes.
Her hearing, a compass rose plotting the positions of people,
The courses of their passing. Her sense of smell so acute
Every garden's location is marked, a capital
Of a foreign country, where she is always welcomed,
As she vividly imagines the memories.

Somewhere

I wish to call this something
That suits my sensibilities.
Not having been too long
In one place, I am at a loss
To know how deep I feel a need
To have belonged from somewhere.
It is important to be from there,
A spot, at times, right down
To the floor boards you can say
You have paced back and forth
Many sleepless nights for no reason.

Being from, seems so much easier
When you must talk about yourself.
For ease, I pick, *The Big Apple*.
It is a lie I use because
It is so easy to get away with.
No one will ever ask if I know
So and so, or is that store where
The low-life's hung still open.
It's just the place for all your fictions
To be born and then get lost in.

Though, it is not inconvenient
To have been from nowhere.
No changes have taken place.
There is no one you must see
To find out what's gone on
Between your going and coming.
You never over stay your welcome.
The extra room in your memory
Can be used to remember things
More important than the streaks
Of light cast by a morning's sunrise
That skipped the waters and bejeweled
Dew hung on marsh grasses
As if a thousand single eyes
Recognized you from somewhere.

The Hunting Blind

With night I lie alone next to a woman
Who casts the shadows of wife and mother;
In the next room children breathe
Like trees, green and sure with sleep.
Above me in the attic, coiled in wakefulness,
Lie the dark animals of memory
That never forget the hunter.

I rise from the world of sleeping figures
Growing smaller and smaller, retreating
Into the night of a closely guarded wood
Where the air is hot and hard to take in
And begin to stalk, following the tracks.
How easy the habits are to trail
Even in the most moonless of nights
Where every sound resembles
The raw intelligence of leaves,
The heart's beat, that terrible silence
Of trembling on the breeze that comes
Face to face with what has been
And always be the question
That has no proper answer.

I try to dream the forest's edge where
I can awaken, like a child, the restless lie.

I try to dream and dream remembering
And remembering claim to know its being.
How desire strips the creature of its nature
So its movements become one within the hunter
As he moves among their kind,
Concealed from what he is, a skin within a skin
Who dreams the beast, its girth of shoulder
Crashing through the underbrush.

Only the hunter knows the wound that does not kill.

The Letter

Brother,
There's a madman lives inside us. He dwells
Deep in the common wilderness we share.
A hermit from all daily thoughts. His madness
Makes him passive to the workings of the stars.

He reads the changes in the weather
In the way the light fails to cast its shadows.
But, in those days, sleepless from the exhaustion
Of his leisure, he takes on the wrestling of desires,
And becomes resolutely sane. Like clockwork,
The ticking presence of his method, axe in hand,
He goes to the clearing he has been making.

Last week he moved south–for three days
The silhouette of ridge along the sky flattened.
Yesterday, he worked in a south by south-east direction
Towards where the sea might have been
Had there been water. He seems to have no mind
In directions. His compass is always spinning.

Today he is headed north. He recognizes the landmarks.
In the 'chock,' 'chock,' 'chock,' that is chopping away
At all that lies between us. When he is done
I wonder by what signs will we know each other then?

Tiny Stories

I did not pray for visions or ask to be
A reliquary of things inside of things,
The movement in the corner of someone's eye,
A pedestrian eclipsed in the rush for day,
Set free from all appointments, a prisoner
Who must find the moment that can replace
The moment lost by hesitation in others.
I close my mind to it all, writing on the air
My censure of a past that will not happen.

Time is made of tiny stories—a lost ticket, laughter
Down the hall, nights spent in stairwells listening
To the conversations of elevators, furniture nailed
To the ceiling of a room, a peculiar noise muffled,
Being a life in someone's nightmare, begging
For water and given sand with lies
Scratched onto the surface of every grain,
Books that cannot be closed without forgetting,
A confession, a puzzle with no solution.

The house of desires has no affinity
For the tactile discernment of reminiscence.
Windows become mirrors, mirrors windows;
Doors walls, walls doors. I pass through
Delicate light confused by its illumination,
Seeking to barter a gentle subtle communion
For an awareness of the dialects of color.
I am mad with a consuming, unruly fever
For a language not yet conceived and born.

Weightlessness

The year sighs
Thru autumn's grace,
Into the aria winter is.
Nothing moves,
Except an illusion of moon
Against almost morning's darkness.
The only sound,
A breathing cold front
Spiraling in.

I close my eyes.
I am in a child's belief
Where birds hang in the air
With night, to wait on
A buoyant first light
To set them free.
Such myths my father rendered,
In his way, not talking
So much as willing,
To let the lessons be
Wonder and surprise.
Later on, older,
Needing proofs I knew
He did not own.

I remember,
A dawning like this.
He stood tall, outstretched,
Pointing at Orion's belt,
'They say up there is weightlessness.'
Anxious to be my own,
I *asked* him how *he* knew?
He folded back into himself
Where he knew I would not go.

Weightlessness continued…

After,
Slow, so slow,
I learned how
To become the man I became.
Thinking each day
How easy it was
To leave behind
That simplistic faith in things
That held me to him.
But now make
His assured silences,

Isolated…

So loud.

Hindsight

Hindsight has nothing
To do with seeing what you did.
It's only looking into the past
Of something that may have happened
And becomes an obsessive trait.

To live like this is my own doing.
No one else can know the need
For finding an answer as I.
A solitude that will not share
Its contemplations with anyone
Lives outside what was experienced,
Alone, with nothing to embrace.

I could give you clues
With which to divert your purpose
And let you leave in a reverie
Bemused with an understanding,
That outstretched arms can gather
Some small part of the corner
Of a world you call a possession
Of a silence all your own. But you
Would not be comforted for long.
Looking back you would begin
To feel that satisfaction as incomplete
And your curiosity feeding upon itself.

But the doors are closed, the windows
Boarded against both looking in
And seeing out. Time has no standard
To unfold and the effigies of what has gone
Flinch and flap on the indolent breezes.

Should Death Arrive Before I Do

Should death arrive before I do,
Ask him to wait for me. I will not
Be long, knowing how much He
Hates to wait, having so much to do.
It must be a great responsibility
Having to account for everyone who's
Inevitable time has come, like Time,
He waits for no man, nor should He.

Tell him how an unusually punctual man
I am. In fact, lacking more social grace
Most times, I'm horribly early. It may
Startle Him and make Him think how
Important the thing that holds me back
Must be. I would imagine He understands
At times there are just priorities that must
Be met: a list I've been crossing off all day.

There is nothing that will clue me into what
His demeanor might be, though seeing Him
Is far less welcomed than having root canal;
I would venture He feels very much disliked.
Still, though there may, in instances, be pain
Before one meets Him, I can't see it in the
Simple crossing over. Just the same if am late
And He impatient, tell Him to go ahead and I
Will be sure to be right behind and catch up
                                    When I can.

Traveling

The train's whistle
Cuts through the heart,
Like a ray of sun through snow.
Somewhere out there,
Beyond the tracks, was a life.
Staring out. The child,
Watching the street,
Exists only in a forever
Of imagination. You are
No longer bound to this place.
It's by chance you are
Only passing through.

Traveling is belonging.
It is a place all its own:
In the beginning is its end;
In its end is the beginning
--A landscape never completed;
The journey, a glancing strike
Of curiosity that remains
Awake and keen. Aware.

The Situation of Gravity
Or,
How Miracles Are Performed

The Situation of Gravity, or How Miracles Are Performed

From somewhere deep inside the Midwest
A woman writes a letter to an afternoon
Radio revival preacher she has been listening to
All her life. She asks him to pray with her.
She asks him to ask Jesus to make her thin.
In her fat womanly voice she says, 'Jesus, please,
Make me thin.' (She pauses. *How to ask*
Without asking?) 'It's been so hard, being fat
Each year, people always laughing
When I try to dance. Never being able to wear
Horizontal stripes. Never dating.
It's been so hard.'

Along the interstate, one evening, a young man
Is driving. (*To someone's heart? Perhaps.*
There is No need to know.) He listens to the radio.
He knows the song. He knows the road.
He takes The turn too tight and meets the night stretching
Out before him, beyond the pull of gravity.

He is airborne.   She is weighted down.

(*How can they ever meet?*)

On the radio, one afternoon, a preacher reads
A woman's letter. He tells his listening audience
That in his hands, he holds a letter from a woman
Who says that Jesus has made her thin.
 'Glory, Glory, Glory!'

If only the young man could have been listening.
Perhaps, as he broke through the safety rails
And left the cry of solid double yellow lines
Behind him, He might have watched for a Goddess
Dancing, slowly rising from the fog of constellations,
Dressed in horizontal stripes, her arms thrown wide
                    To greet him like a God.

The Painter

(After, Andrew Wyeth)

Through his door a woman has come hurriedly,
Her apron held up to her face to wipe the tears
In reddened eyes. Following close, a man
In faded, stained overalls, holds his felt hat
In his hand, careens through the too short opening
For his frame. It is everything we need to know.
The rest is conjecture. We must imagine.

In another space, the window open, thin curtains
Billow, float on the warm wafts of unbreathed air.
Part of one more summer passing over waves
Of grasses in a fallow field. An old man, his face
Furrowed by a hold a landscape has on his heart,
Enters on aching legs to take a seat at the table.
He looks into the breeze passing beyond the earth.

Other rooms and other places are filled
With anticipation of things already happened.
We cannot help but contemplate the possibilities
For shades living out their pallet born lives
We do not see so much as we are drawn into.
Asked to participate in emotions we are not sure of
But recognize as our own, we take part because
They exist in a world we want to go on forever.

Here, is caught all that is America passed by.
Anxieties come home to rest in yellow-ochers
Browns, blues and the whitest whites, taupe,
Like quiet cares blended onto the background
In our unconscious, where we believe we can
Lean our head out a favored window
Hoping to call someone home for a supper
That simply does not happen anymore.

I Swear To God

I swear to god, that if God existed he would find
In me a match despite my size and seeming mortality.
But I'd aim to have it out with him just to set things
Straight. No parting seas, or burning bush, tablets
Set in stone, nor trumped up martyrdoms would
Sway me into adopting a more humble stance.

Bare knuckles, kicks and bites, a gouged eye or two;
I'm not beyond pulling hair or a beard now and then.
Surprise will be my ally. How could he think some one
Would just have had enough of being in a master plan.
I thought Herman would have been the one, but he chose
Moby Dick instead and ended his days trapped in that
Diminishing refrain, *I would prefer not to*. Piss off! I say.

I am well aware of who the betting money's on. I know
It's a fool's errand. But here I'll stand and wait until
You know what freezes over. And if he's not man enough
I imagine a lightning strike will set me right and teach me
To know my place—six by three into the earth. But at least
I'll know I was here, which is more than many can say.

Refuge

What can absolve us from the curfews
Your heart has set with a bruising tongue?
In a language I once knew as valid,
The paths of desire have been misquoted,
Held captive, twisted and nuanced,
Into chance and changed values of which
My mocked deafness made me unaware.

I see your dance in finger print patterns
Marking the boundaries of your beliefs..
They line the lobbies, stairs and hallways
Like sentinels accentuating your accusations
Keeping love's specter a prisoner inside
A room filled with chaos, boredom and dust.

How can I change your façade to forgiveness
While memory's unkind mask remains?
How did you become what you are now
A partisan of sabotage and guerilla raids,
Raising havoc in every direction to find
Where my exiled heart is still beating?

I could begin by razing your city
In a predatory communion of search and destroy:
Block by block, house to house combat;
A catastrophe's inexpedience swept away
By denying the body counts of remorse,
Where the wounded are no better off than the dead.

In the end does any of this matter?
The hollowness I clothe and feel
Reasons against all that's passed.
I can see the only distance between us
Is in accepting our misunderstandings
Insecurities, regrets and doubts
As all parts of the refuge that is love.

Balance

We are never sure if we are starting over
Or just beginning. The transient nature of life
Perches us on a delicate set of scales
Each moment, a thousand possibilities.
Unsure of the processes of choice we begin
To cultivate the person we imagine ourselves
To be. In the beginning we believe
What we say, and hope to say what we believe.
But the contexts we encounter are fragile
In their composure and relative, like
The smeared landscape seen through a window
Of a train. We only see the world racing
Past us, until we take a seat, and look,
To find we are the ones moving; but where?

Too soon an atmosphere of being
Owned by our desires wraps around us
Demanding attention like a child.
What was initially a determination
To merge our needs, hopes and anticipations
Seems tenuously tipping, about to evaporate
Into infinity. What we see in the mirror
Has no breath and is the past, always behind
The perfect ticking timing metronome
Of our hearts. That is where the key lies.
Finding balance against anxiety.
Embracing the chance to see
That our hearts are made of millions of lives
And courage to go into what has always been
There waiting. The unknown.

Penelope

A fading fresco from 79 A.D. Pompeii, saved from pumice
And ash to let light breathe life again into a more ancient
Greek, a woman passing delicate, painted plaster fingers
Over the heat-crazed cracks cutting the strings of a lyre,
Playing notes no one but those dead now hear.

Could this be the famed, prescient Penelope of Ithaki
Before us, off from her loom of deceit, while suitors
Stupefied by wine from her cellars and their bravado,
Sleep, unmindful of the Fates, below in the great hall?

The many years in fidelity of watching, wait worn,
Longing for Odysseus to take her in his arms,
Not wanting to hear the lies spun about his hardships;
But only, to firmly woo her under a night sky full of stars.

Can she know, deep in her heart of hearts, be sure,
Of unfaithfulness with goddesses? Would she pretend
To believe when he swore of spells that had bewitched him,
To share the love he had vowed to all others to deny?

How did it feel to one who bore him his child, now a man,
Kept his house, fed him meals as if he himself divine,
To know, those ten years growing older, it was mere
Adventure kept him gone, not just the anger of the gods?

Put off, by memory, from music meant to soothe her, alone,
Did she lay down her instrument without remorse, or regrets
And turn back to the day's woven tapestry set tight on the loom
To slowly undue a weaving she had not wanted to begin?

Annotations

The sound of laughter
From the courtyard filtered up,
In through the window of his study.
The day was unseasonably warm.
Now and then he would write
In a small hand some note or reference
In the margin of the book.
More laughter,
Louder now, with more voices.
He recognized the lilt in hers.
He knew it would not be.
He closed the book
And sat back, removed his glasses
Balanced their weight in his hand.
A sigh, as inaudible
As the small pain he felt,
Escaped his lips.
He smiled.

Circumstantial Evidence

The commotion of the city is quickly becoming filled
In the conversation of doors ajar and stairwells.
The neighbors argue Philosophy like recipes,
Cups of flowers, place settings on the holidays.
The temples open. Mass celebrated and the speaking
In tongues falls on deaf ears. What is left of desire
Is in ruins and divided among the refugees of boredom,
The guilds of lovers and tourists who populate
The doorways like rain. The toll booths fill with credit.
The price of everything is going up. We are as secure
As luggage left behind on the platform in the care
Of a stationary traveler. As our imagination moves
We feel accused of never having gone far enough.

We look for payment in a broader experience owed us:
The backs of heads become faces, and the landscapes
Through the windows smear. What was once the real
Is something else we are not sure of. Each compartment
Is filled with it too. Taking part in the gray areas
Of communion with ourselves, in the movement
Before leaving. we faintly glimpse the color
Of the atmospheres we breathe, and understand the need
To fix upon some object, let its attention place us

In our movement through so that time begins to pass again.
All that's left, all the rest of what there is lies
In the cities where the noise hangs on the necklace of sleep
While the night leaks out into the darkness like a convict of belief
On the escaping streets. We learn to live like architecture.
Even the phases of the moon become something more.
The physics of the heart are clear then fogged in by formulae.
What was once a season set with dreams transforms
The world into a weightless nightmare. Sleep shakes its coat
For something to articulate. The words get caught.
The landlord allows the rent to slip. Friends recall us
In other situations. We allow ourselves to think
That if we have a round trip ticket in our possession
Then perhaps the journey is redundant after all.

Things Left Behind

The long hallway ended at the inevitability of thought,
Chained to a heart of darkness fear. The floors
Were a cluttered disaster of debris, dismantled,
Dreams awaiting a closure within persistent waking.
The questions about noises in the next room
Answered by scratches on the window.
Conversation was discussion. Discussion,
Always monologue. There was chaos for breakfast.
Un-mailed postcards for lunch. Dinner always random.

Waiting was recreation--its injuries repeated, gained
Fluency, an outside world seen through
A mask worn too often for survival and became
A revolving door of options in which choice
Had ceased to be among them.

The weather was an encyclopedia of expenditures
Required to go from one room to the next.
Quiet, experienced as an emotion
Written out with repetition, a thousand times
'*I must be… I must be… I must …,*' on both sides
Of a page from yesterday's newspaper, torn in half.
Language, a commodity which time was bartered for.
Memory, rewritten. What was written, revised daily.

In the close quartered room which sanctuary visited,
Under the bed, behind the unused suitcase, is a book
Filled with drawings in pencil and awash
In secreted colors. It was a talisman of coveted things
Pressed between the pages: the feathers of small birds
From the rusted escape; thumb-sized patterned paper
Torn from walls of rooms in a decaying place; a folded,
creased torn magazine photo of an erupting volcano,
Angry with lava; an inset map detail of clustered islands,
'*The Encantadas,*' that came from a book taken back;
The flattened, dry blossom, which long ago, was a part of
A now dead bouquet.

Older now, inured to the hostilities of days
Melded into a collage of rehearsed nightmares,
He prepares to leave, retrieves the book,
Thumbs through the pages of days and nights
Smudged with the age of captured occurrences,
Then puts it where it will never be found again.

Some talismans are meant to attract
The gaze of pains and their darker scars;
Entice them with offerings, then ensnare
And hold them, so they do no harm again.

It is not the only thing left behind.

The Paper Iris

Every year the delicate paper iris
Blooms once and lasts but hours.

Our histories have unfolded in chaos
Before our eyes instead of through them.
We look but fail to see the repetitions.
We carry ourselves like catastrophes,
Shadows of failed vows and, broken oaths.
Our promises remain chrysalis woven,
Unwilling to emerge into the light.
There are no moments of indiscretions,
There is only indiscretion in everything.

The sky does not explode because
Too many birds take flight at once.

Our past cannot be caressed
Into façades of bemusing affectation,
Seeking to seduce a better future.
We cannot make arrangements
With the clouds for our desires,
Or think rehearsing the sound of water
Can quench our thirst with imagination.

We move in space between heaven
And earth unaware how fragile
Their balance is affected by our passing.
At some point we must let
The real world introduce itself
In order to learn who we are,
Show us what we can be,
Allowing the tempo of our lives,
To match the cadence of our hearts.

Pablo's Muse

In 1900, Paris, there was
A young woman of the streets
Who sat for me in exchange
For half my lunch. I spoke
No French, to understand
Wasn't hard; she had to slip
Her robe, I only had to paint,
But when she did and I began,
My brush had a life of its own,
Yellow-ochre, burnt sienna, azure
Her eyes and a smile
To make even Leonardo sigh.

That winter, Max and I so poor
And freezing; if it burned
It did, and canvases too.
I remember at the last,
The best work I ever did,
Took my heart with it
        Up in smoke.

The Magician or, a History from the Mid-West

(For, Mac Hammond)

It's been said that he'd been quite common, a magician
Slight in his sleight of hand pulling rabbits out of hats,
Ping-Pong balls and aces from the thin air. Flowers
From a glass of milk and the clichéd colored scarves
Of silk that went red, to green, to yellow, to dual blue
As usual, turned into a dove that flew into the rafters
Of a hundred mid-west towns and whistle stops,
Until the show was toured-out and through.

Then once, back in Iowa, at the 1938 State Fair,
There, beneath the flag-topped tents
That fluttered as blue as the big sky was,
When the audience seemed entertained and still,
He asked for some assistance. She volunteered.
She moved toward the stage with a limp.
He reached out his hand to help her up and
Only slightly touched her. The crowd blinked once.
The weather changed.
And the girl in her crippled walk became a rain
Skipping the wheat fields and the flatlands
Traveling east beyond the dirt roads out-of-town.

A week later, in Wichita, on a railroad siding
He barely brushed against a man who changed
Into a field of Prairie White Touch Me Not's
Whose yellow fingers swooned in summer showers.
Word went around. His fame began to grow.
Finally the tabloids picked him up
As he swept with transformation through the heartlands.

A mailman in Topeka became a race horse.
In Cedar Rapids a house wife became swift rapids
On a river that had formerly been her lover.
In St. Louis a group of children were seen
To take the flight of geese for fact
In their migration from the schoolyard.

The Magician continued…

Notoriety pressed in. Recognized on every street,
The public clambered near him to be touched.
He found less time to sleep, relax, to be himself,
To be by himself. Until, he felt beside himself.
That last night in his dressing room, his face bathed
In the bathos powdered glow of the make-up mirror's lights.
He gazed into the dulling eyes and their reflection
Reached out towards him. He slid his hand
Across the glass as if to set the image free.
Felt a gentle tug on his lapel and fell into a wave,
Overturning into ocean surf forever.

What You Get

'You get what anybody gets.
He said, 'you get a lifetime.'
God almighty I don't know
How many times I've had
To listen to him say it. Over
And over, again and again,
Like some fortune cookie mantra.
In all that time, apart from
The obvious, it never made
An ounce of sense to my way
Of thinking.

One day, a month ago.
As I was coming out of the deli,
I looked up and saw a crowd
Of people standing on a corner.
Suddenly from nowhere
A man bolted like lightning
Into the walkway where a kid
Had wandered into against the light.
It was dusk, the light was bad,
The truck slammed its brakes,
They were both gone that quick..

I still can't have it make a difference
In my life, in how I live.
But, at least now when he says it,
I understand what he means.

What Whispers

There is so much that we would rather
Have left unknown. It whispers to us
In our sleep. Something half dreamt,
Taking the form of a stranger,
Crosses our path and is gone. Our days
Refine themselves around us in conversation
Or, in glimpses of a past we do not recognize
But know as ours. There is rain outside
Bringing nothing but confusion with it.

It is not a thing to be boxed and hidden.
It is a part of you leaning, pressing forward
On your shoulder, watching everything you do
In your *secret world*. Nothing is ever yours
Alone. All the time you wonder
If you should expect something to happen:
Stepping off a curb that isn't there
Would almost be welcomed to stop
The tightness you feel, like small pockets
Of dense winter air, impossible to breathe.

Change paws the window like an indigent
We refuse to see and pull the curtains closed.
There is a desire to be better, but more
Enamored with the process than we are
Of any real change. Our self-importance fed,
The absurd is condoned by absurdity
Until one day finds us in between tracks
Watching a train speeding towards us.
We wake to find it still coming on.
Out of synch with time we are frozen,
Not by fear, but a ludicrous curiosity
In the vanishing point perspective of the rails
Into darkness where shadows won't dissolve.

What Whispers continued…

There is no logic, no equation, no incantation.
Explanations are occurrences like face cards
At Black-Jack, there are only so many to play.
We can only wear the *Emperor's clothes*
For so long, before we realize they are not *new.*
Our lives and living them are all there is.
Self-reflection requires no condemnation
Of failings or fears. What whispers to us
Is who we really are and sometimes as simple
As throwing back the curtains and opening
                                    The window.

The Way Water Freezes

The Way Water Freezes

I will learn
To love you slow,
The way water freezes,

Crystalline skim ice
Between cold air
And still liquid below.

I will thicken
Over you,
Encasing each
Of our afterthoughts,

Aware of their presence,
The way I know you

In a room with lights out,
Solitary, pooled
In one place
Ready to flow
Through my fingers
In the dark.

We can
Mingle our breath clouds
And leave no fingerprints
On the blue ice.

Let our movements
Be one thing

And I will learn
To love
You

The way water freezes.

Astronomy

The truth about the way that she appeared
Remains a mystery to me. Though I read
Through much of the night sky,
Like some acolyte of the zodiac, I can fit
No constellations to its happenstance,
No rhyme scheme verbal magic to unfold
Even an adumbration of precursory events
For the moment to occur. And yet its fact
Is that I was there and she was there
In completely varied orbits, catching
At each other with independent pulls
Of gravitational attraction against odds
Astronomical in proportion when set against
The everyday patterns of life on earth.
But calculations cannot plumb the depths
Of how hidden love can make itself known
In the second it takes a star to burst
And make a galaxy all its own
Just in her saying, '*Oh, we've met before.*'

A Mask

If you will wear a mask for me, I will become
Unbound personalities of fragrant passions
Who wait at every corner that you pass
Following the map of misspoken histories,
Left in place of a bowl of paper irises
That I'll use to leave you clues concerning
All the things we know but never learn about.

If you will wear a mask for me, I will walk
Across the skylines of a hundred sleeping
Cities and replace all your chandeliers
With changing cloud forms stolen from Tibet
And illuminate the puzzled look you give
To visitors who cannot translate the nuances
Of frescos painted in a pallet gone berserk..

If you will wear a mask for me, I will gather
The things you fear the most and sink them
Between the Bosporus and the Dardanelles
And make believe I've traveled to the moon
Just to see you from a distance in extreme,
And still be back in place to disguise the hours
We lose wondering what we need of time at all.

If you will wear a mask for me, I will promise
To be the one who gently takes it from you
And never forget I am with who you really are.

Night

I am wrapped in night like music waiting
To begin a next piano movement
By Poulenc.
Beauty is in the next room.
Desire, one floor down.
The stars have been sweating days
For this moment to occur.

This is an open City filled with lights.
But it is in the dark
I want to have you, lust
Filling the air
With scents of our bodies barely touching,
Yet enjoined as one joint of flesh,
So if the world ever have a need for us
It will not recognize our single shadow,
Pass by
And believe the rumors
Spread in bistros.
Of how the dream-world, jealous,
Came out of hiding
And stole back with us
Behind the daylight,
Never to be seen again.

Lace

Your eyes see things in me
I could only hope to know.
In my world of madness,
Selfishness and cynical disregard,
Not uttering a word you show
How small a shadow I cast
And how much more of living
My arms might hold.
It is not something
I am always enamored of,
To shed old skin for new
Does not come without
The price one pays in fear to trust.

So I watch you move
From place to place,
Your faith upheld
By the same strength
That allows a dragonfly to glide on
Wings made just of lace
And wonder…

Lunar Seas

I woke to a thousand moons
Waxing in the night; faint
Crescent smiles dusting earth
With light. I wanted you to see;
To show you, to gift to you
The luminescence of reflection
That was holding up the sky.
But sleep had spun you
A cocoon of dreams
I hesitated to unravel,
To intrude upon a reverie.

It's hard to choose:
A dream, or illusion.
One's a carousel's promise-painted
Ponies circling a calliope;
The other, a river
Passing slow, deep, wide,
With swirling eddy's, and
A current's pull to sea.

So I imagined for you
A flight of mirrored birds,
Weaving in and out of light
Just above cratered surfaces
And a thousand lunar seas.

The Blue Trees

In the morning you watch
The blue trees' shadow
Shorten over the drifts
Of winter as the sun rises,
Until their contrast is dark
And brittle beneath them.

The surprise of daylight's
Secret is never lost on you.
In the ways you move in
And out of it, the season's
Freshness continually
Whispers its transience.

The day's warming
Makes the snow heavy
And bows the blue branches
Of the blue trees, their tips
Touching the ground
To sweep at the matchstick
Tracks of birds that feast
On the seeds you scatter
With delicate sighing hands
On the small wind of air.

Star's Light

What is it that you cannot find
Hidden in the folded imprint
The sun leaves behind on the air
That seems so important now?

Your gestures, like an insurrection
Of willows in wind before rain,
Assume they control the clouds.
I can and would deny you nothing.

With you, I am shadow cut loose
From substance, absorbing
It's likeness from its own animation.
Aware all essence is tentative.

But there is no use not to imagine
I am a small sound traveling
The length on the map of your body.
Vibrating against your presence.

Boisterous, ribald, calming, poetic,
All of my voices at once one thing,
Celebrates your existence with echoes
Of a star's light long after its source
                         Has darkened.

Rain

The color of the rain desires our attention.
You ignore fact and fictively reach
Into the box always kept nearby and remove
An allegory of this morning's near perfect
                              Soft asylum.

There are no mistaken promises hidden within
Its folds. The allusion of your body moves from
Shadow to shadow, a slow stream moving through
A valley of iris, their blue, white, purple reflecting
                              Surface, rippled.

I dip my face into your waters and let the coolness
Cleanse my eyes. When I open them I see you are
What you were, what you have always been to me,
The persuasive whisper in my ear giving our world
                              A secret voice.

For you, my touch is a prayer written down
On small candle flames when my thoughts go
To another place. You are so patient of the way I am,
Your lights never diminish, marking our time
                              A forever.

With you, I have no need of memory. It only hinders
My imagining what you do when we are not together.
But, we are never parted because in my heart
A piece of yours makes mine beat to the breathing
                              And tempoed rain.

The Peddler

The restlessness of my love,
Makes my language mute.
So, I travel the towns of your heart,
A peddler in emotion. I try to explain
With a dumb show of curiosities
And objects I pull from the sack
I carry. A burden I bear for lack
Of words for your ears, in the hope
You will see what I mean.

There is no other course
Than to chance in the essence
That makes a thing, in presenting
How it dovetails with another
To form a thoughtful syntax:

The feather from an angel's flight, a rock,
A rusted lock, a watch waiting for time,
The shadow outlines of ancient irises
Pressed into clay, hardened to stone,
The deeper I dig.

But, I know no matter.
In the end, all I have to show
Are things, alive with meanings,
Inside my head, subjective and subject
To interpretations that vary from intention.

When all is ended and my tale shown
I have no speech, no voice to tell,
How your ocean washes over my shoreline,
In wave after, after wave, after wave.

You're Earth

Your love has the constancy
Of the earth turning on axis.
I know your Norths from
Your Souths. They move
Languidly in space made for you.

But it is your Easts and Wests
That redefines my imagination
With their delight of speed, revolving
Past the sun in days and nights
I gave up counting because
It diminished the great joy I found
Listening to the clouds
As they embrace the terrain
   Of your laughter.

When I Think of You

I wonder can you feel me
When I think of you,
Early in the morning
When I stop what I am at,
Make that moment
Yours alone as if it were
Something you could see,
Hold and unwrap.

I know I am far from
The person you first met
But then, we are both far
Away from whom we were.
It took strength in reserve
To weather our lives.

Shadows are always present.
Their genesis is formed
From light, so they must
Be good in ways
If only to mark the sun.

I know how very much I wish
You could learn
To love me as I am
Just as much as I try
To be someone you can love.

Sometimes I simply
Don't know how.
But if you could feel me
When I think of you
You would feel me
Almost all the time.

The Importance of Wonder

The Importance of Wonder

A child may be told the night sky is spun with paper,
Believe its future written forever on it by the stars,
Then see it washed away in the bittersweet of dawn.
Though I am older and such stories I've left behind
There still beats a child's curiosity inside me
Always open to see the world in awe and wonder.

Who hears the melodies of wintered roots holding tight
Into the soil as spring blesses their resistant fragility?
If I stroke the undersides of leaves in autumn, bright
With season, before they fall onto the ground,
Could they tell me there are places in the heart
We never know are there, with capacity meant
For more than merely living only for ourselves?

Who can say they have witnessed the shadows
Passion casts without accusing desire of selfishness?
Why is it we stand empty while around a corner
The tiny particles of larger loves may wait?

I have found true silence among small stems swaying
On afternoon wind in rhythm of a moment's pain.
In a world where trees, unlike men, die standing,
I maintain an acute nostalgia for the present
Before it becomes the past and leads to thinking
Of the future as a delicate point for indecision.

Without becoming patron saints of discarded things
What questions are we prepared to let go unasked?
Speaking for myself I will go without applause.
Still finding meanings in the smallest things,
All doubts shouted down by echoes of assurance.
I became the man I am because I never held
Any stars above me responsible for my life.

I say, let us start again, heart to heart, once more
Balancing questions on our walking sticks, filling
The strength our arms have left with only wonders.

The Beauty of Water

The unbroken light of surface tension,
Élan of possibilities,
Unfolds, retreats, unfolds fully now.
Caress, the first touch, a kiss-gentle
Thought of yearning, then satisfies itself
By turning on an off-tonal pause
Marries faith, brushes innocence.
Wishes chance believing a naturalness
In circulation—in its circularity,
                    Completion.

A Word

(After Wallace Stevens)

I buried a word in Tennessee,
Its likeness had not been heard,
In a fallow field left untouched
And in mute listening around it.
A tree grew and wild it was.

It made look the lay of land
No longer simply flat with
Grasses, or without sound.
It became of all the air,
Siren called to that place.
Its flowerings bore tender fruit
And tasted of all I knew
        From everywhere.

A Time of Dreams

There are rules in dreams that must not be broken:
Never do things in threes; don't ask a soul for directions;
Take care not to stand in a shadow's shadow, then
Only the breath of moths can save you from disbelief.

Meet me where the long light ends uncertain
And the sound of talking bends like glass and metal.
There I will be standing shadow free, alone, whistling
A tune you will recognize yet have never heard.

I will make excuses for you, no one will mind,
Or pay any notice by the way you are clothed.
Be sure to bring a book that can turn into a bird.
It may be crucial to the outcome in close arrangements.

There will be no time for the amenities of introductions.
Names here have the value of paper hats in rain.
You will be known by how adept you are to translate
What unfolds before you in a language of knotted rope.

Here, it is dark with suspicion, full of dangerous small lies.
I am watching for you, lighting candles along the way,
Leading into a time of dreams, the Yaquis called *Alcheringa*,
Where your memory awakens in the sleep you will forget.

A Frost-Straw Colored Sky

I can think of things to keep me here
In this spot of snowed-in and forgotten
Wilderness, not really so far from town.

All time waits and hangs above the ground,
Mingling with close hushed living sounds,
Gathering where branch meets trunk
Among the trees. It is where all secrets go.

In that one thing there is enough attraction
Alone to make me wish that a day could be
More a week of days to stay.

I would amble amid the varied species
Looking for hidden things I put away
And don't remember anymore. Though even
If I found them within spruce, or pine, or birch
What purpose would they serve me now
At this late hour of a frost-straw colored sky
Signaling darkness to take dominion here.

For me, it means, I might return another time.
But now, I go back home leaving more
Than my meandering tracks to melt behind.

Feeding Fish

He comes here to feed the fish.
In suit, tie, pants pressed, shoes shined.
Reaches into a brown paper bag for
Small pieces of bread he thoughtfully rolls
Between finger and thumb, throws
To the throng of turning, twisting, swimming,
Golden-orange fish that have lived forever
In this pond. Every day for an hour
Rain or shine, snow or wind, and heat.

If I were to believe in a God
I imagine Him a man like this.
A God with so many things to mind,
Prayers and supplicants to answer
While He watches what His creations do.
He sees the cruelest of cruelties done
With His name on men's lips.

He also sees when men are true,
Noble beyond what He'd imagined.
In spite of that He cannot be everywhere
To do all that believers expect of Him.

I think He would find some spot
To not think about any of the world.
Where nothing is asked or expected.
A calming place, quite quiet, away,
The only concern, a pond of fish
Hungry for tiny balls of bread.

This Man

Films and streets, schools and towns, capital cities,
A car and highway, Boston
To Seattle and back, currency tendered,
All bear his name. His face jack-hammer chiseled
Into a mountain's side.

Today, what are we to make of him,
Our *moderness* so removed,
From the debt we owe forever?

I have been to *The Memorial*, touched the giant marble;
In size so metaphoric, its solidity so cold--so unlike
The man, so less than what he was.

From his final place of rest I have a stone;
I've stood on hallowed ground. Where men died,
He renewed,
'The last best hope on earth.'

The books that attempt to explain his life, I read over again,
Always hesitating to begin—knowing how they must end:

In a boarding house room too crowded, on too small a bed,
In a pocket of an ill-fit suit, a spare pair of spectacles,
A carefully folded Confederate five dollar bill.

If a *butterfly effect* has any meaning in the repercussions
Such small occurrences have, I wonder then,
How many butterflies took flight at once,
To make it possible for *this man* to be born?

Of Song Light

Sometimes song light, it can be so soft
Coming through a window, it may seem
As though a close kept secret, it's fragile
Nature undiscovered by the outside.

I see your words as shadows dimmed,
A voice bent in resignation, dissolves
Before being spoken and heard and makes
Known the hold longing to be broken.

A life no longer continuing to grow older
Becomes a lie, told over and over again,
A confidence for you to keep, another lie,
Until no home can be just rooms filled with hurt.

I will build you rooms of paper song birds
Whose nests have all been burnt by pain,
Yet still sing, to show you how the heart
Can heal in time by remembering to forget.

Perhaps minutes of awareness will lapse
Into hours, then days, weeks into years, when
The all the house becomes uncluttered,
Your words heard as songs when spoken.

Sometimes song light can be so softening.
It makes its way through thickest walls,
Illuminates and denies the dark of surrender
In showing the world still lives outside.

Rivers

Beneath their unreflective surfaces are currents,
Not quite hypnotic, not quite benign,
That pick at our sin of curiosity.

Though named on maps, charted, explored,
They are not things.
They are themselves, events taking place,
Engaged in changing;
Floating all incidents of living lives,
The dead thoughts, along from head waters,
Miles down to silted deltas, memories,
Now detritus, diluted in salted waters,
Washed to sea.

We think we want to watch them,
But it is their nature to make us feel the urge,
The haunting hunger, a need to know
What meanings they express.

In a language of erosion
Carving great canyons from ancient rock,
And the patterns left on farm fields
When full of rainfall or snowmelt they overflow,
Washing away banks
To inundate the land around for miles.
The secrets of rebirth bleeding,
Soaked into the ground,
Waiting to be seeded, to wash away once more..

In nature
They stay the same. Moving, flowing, going down,
Always new water moves past us,
Always the same river coursing--a moment
Never repeated, always taking place,
An anomaly, carrying our senses with safety
And still unstable.

No matter what we think, they stir an ancient need
In us, to be placed as firmly
As we can be and yet move in our imagination
With the currents,
Around the next bend.

That One Moment

There was no more need of saints
So she wore the clothing of a ghost;
Each tear she shed opening new sorrows
The sparrows of remorse flew thru.

With love, his life became perfect.
But without yearning, he pined away,
Sought comfort in a past of weeds
And soon not even they would grow.

The song of morning is
In its importance of wonder.
The tune of mid-day lies
About tomorrow's love of night.

The lullaby of evening turns
On simple words of phrasing.
The canticle of midnight echoes
In the hollowness of the unfulfilled.

There are moments when we enter
A place for the first time in our lives
And know we've been there before.
Or, felt the stranger in our own scenery.

We forget how much is needed
To keep the shadow plays of life's lies,
Believable enough to fool those we cast
And seem invisible to our own eyes.

No matter who you are, it occurs.
Life freezes in a liminal moment.
A slice of time so thin it doesn't pass;
It just is and we understand it.

The meaning, its reason, the beauty
Of where we were before we knew
And nothing will ever be so lighted
Than the lifetime we let slip away.

The Color of the Clouds

Today the color of the clouds is anxious,
Somehow disenchanted with the memory
Of the sky. Birds sense a disturbance
In the air, their natural navigation
Needs a thought they do not possess.
Everything feels it is waiting. The wild
Grasses have stopped growing.
The trees are in contemplation,
The always passionate brush subdued.
The few flowers here have halted opening
As if the day were not happening
And their blooming be inconsequential.

The earth itself makes no sound, slows
In rotation on its axis, revolves in friction
Around the sun. The oceans are becalmed,
Refuse to tide. Winds become stationary,
Lay into a weightless whispering silence
Muffling the land with a passionate plea.

Miles away a city is laughing, as only cities
Can do, oblivious to the nature of disaster
                    Nature is going through.

What Angels Must Endure

I watch school children under surveillance
By birds of tendered mercy swirling overhead
Marking currents in the air. Underneath
A café awning a man and a woman, twice his age,
Attempt to not be interested in taking advantage
Of what each lacks and wants from the other.

An old woman sits waiting for a bus. One comes,
Yet, she stays seated on the bench, smiles to those
Getting off to turn left or right,
Down or up the block, ignore her.
Her legs are too short; she sways them
Back and forth, as if on a swing trying
To make her body arc into heaven.

A man across the street sees an angel sitting
On the steps leading up to his flat.
He is not surprised. He sits, hands the angel
The Op-Ed. section of the paper. He takes sports.
Into the first paragraph on the second page
The angel curses vehemently out loud.
It seems, the man and I are the only ones
Who notice. Perhaps, are the only ones
Who see the wings shivering,
In anger and frustration.

What if God's punishment, when an angel
Commits one of *those sins* church-goers know about,
Is to make them one of *us*, merely mortal.
It must be an awkward thing,
Losing their heavenly nuance, their celestial essence,
Their left-handed apotheosis,
To be looked down upon.

I look at the rectangular clock across the street.
Garish orange-red LED numbers scream,
You are two hours late!
You said you would come today.
Should I leave?
If you would only ask me to,
I would wait. I would say,
I will wait for you. If it takes forever,
I will wait...

94.

Summer Dreams

Seasons for all themselves don't mean
What they once did. I've not grown
Out of them, rather more into and a part
Of them with a deepening I've not had.
Not to be dramatic, only matter of fact.
A time when each season meant differences
In things needing to be done is done for me.

Those needings now need to be hired out
To those whose labor is not tenuous
But filled with stamina and a resilience
More nimble than my unsteady willingness
To mount a ladder and repair a rotted soffit.
I am not enfeebled by a long way yet. It's just
My work's more now a tooled thought inside.

I.

Autumn is my season of perfect cadences.
In it the heart and mind are at peace.
The slender line of equinox orchestrates
In harmony circumspect participation
Of the four elements that make us part of
An earth fully aware the year is growing late.
Each day a ballet full of import in the air.
Walking, my feet in step with my breathing.

The feel of the first chill-quicken'd bite
In my lungs, holds my concentration close
To what matters–The wideness of the sky,
The attitudes of clouds, the 'V' of flocks flowing
Rather than just in flight, how trees enflamed
Allow a lone evergreen among them to be seen,
The moment, at sunset, when the countryside
Gives the day over to night in sighs
And all the secret names of things are revealed
Then quickly forgotten by the feel of a world
About to relax and make itself ready.

Summer Dreams continued…

II.

Winter has become a year all its own.
It tastes on my tongue of a cello
Playing cascades of suites by Bach,
Continuing one after another without stop,
Each deep lowing expresses the joy
Of a universe still expanding in awe.
Yet, still I'm rooted firm to earth's orbit,
Knowing it would be simple to only let go
And suddenly traveling at light's speed,
Leave all fears behind, bound by gravity.

I think it's what it must have been like
To be Einstein embraced in his reveries,
Questioning the knowns and doubts,
Accepting the unknown and finally,
Having no doubt about coming back,
Slipped the thin atmosphere surrounding
The world delicately drifting in space.

III.

Spring's a flowery mutation all primed up;
A glandular mix of the sacred, the profane
And the pagan; Mardi gras madness—beads
Thrown out to bearing breasts with drunken ease;
Carnival gluttony stumbling into Lenten ash, and
Sacrifice. Ending lined up for the confessional
Ritual of Good Friday, still hungry yet, for more.

Yes, the rest's more like a note left by winter,
The ground saturated with meltdown, into mud;
For me a season of cynics and sarcastic smiling.
When I was young in the sixties and it was all
For politics and sex, love bruising imaginations
Cut to the heart with the hot knife of living,
All caught up in the under currents of renewal
Expecting the world would change by our love.

Though, too, to be honest, my appreciation of
This season, is how it binds the rest with promise.
Always, some part of its fertile dance is woven
Into the cloth of days unfolding of what's to be;
Always, with the thread of hopes to come.

IV.

Summer's world is seen from the pitcher's mound
Long before the crowd arrives. Slightly raised,
Closer to Home than any base, surrounded
By the green grass and raked red clay of possibility.
It is warm roundness and all light rolled out
Into lengths of days. An awakening of all there is;
Opens with clear fields of vision, mowed wind gusts
And dark thunder. A dry in your throat that is not
Thirst, but unquenchable anticipation.

Summer is body time – inside, outside, under
The fingernails dirty. It is Walt Whitman singing
America, while imagining the sweating bodies
Of young men, watching them swim naked,
Diving off a Brooklyn pier. It is a season
Demanding no quarter and giving none back
Except the secrets of Pleasure's alchemy
Turning spun gold into the smell of memories.

It is a world of short close nights tipping
On a horizon's infinity, gentle and tender. Full
Of all one can take from this earth if one chose
To leave it-- more than, much more than that.
It is the season we first learn how dreams
Become the things they are, books opening,
Revealing every page at once; all the things
We can do and cannot do and can do them anyway.
Above all other importants. Above all else,
Summer dreams it is summer; it dreams itself.
What it is about, with a great consciousness
—All of its sinews, bones, muscles and blood in focus,
To see the object of all its exertions at night's end
And the next day's beginning; deep breaths filling
The heart, mind and soul with a pure, deep sleep;
The un-desperate, quiet sleep of summer dreams.

About the Author

K. A. Brace is 61, lives in Nashville, Tennessee with his three dogs and four cats. He is a graduate of The State University of New York at Buffalo where he received both a Bachelor and Masters of Arts degree in English. While at the University he worked with Mac Hammond and Irving Feldman and received the Arthur Axelrod Award for Poetry. After graduating he entered the hospitality industry and did not write for the next 35 years during which time he always considered himself a poet stating that "a poet is one who has written a poem and may never write another."

Coinciding with his turning 60, he began writing again and is in the midst of finishing his seventh collection of poetry. He works assiduously for at least 10-12 hours, 7 days a week at his writing. To Travel Without a Map is his first publication of a book length collection. His style is eclectic and his interest in modern myths and the tiny filaments of our humanity that connects us to one another are the centerpieces of his work. His poems are always surprising both in their crafting and their messages. He considers himself a 'readers' poet.

CPSIA information can be obtained at www.ICGtesting.com
Printed in the USA
LVOW04s1845070715

445299LV00032B/2453/P